URBAN LEOPARDS OF JHALANA

URBAN LEOPARDS OF JHALANA

SOHAM CHAKRABORTY

NIYOGI BOOKS

Published by
NIYOGI BOOKS
Block D, Building No. 77,
Okhla Industrial Area, Phase-I,
New Delhi-110 020, INDIA
Tel: 011-26818960, +91 7428978881
Email: niyogibooks@gmail.com
Website: www.niyogibooksindia.com

Editor: Zinnia Sengupta
Design: Shashi Bhushan Prasad

ISBN: 978-81-19626-02-1
Publication: 2025

Every effort has been made to ensure the accuracy of the information presented in this book. The images used in this book come from either the public domain or from the public commons, unless otherwise stated.

Printed at Niyogi Offset Pvt. Ltd., New Delhi, India

For my parents, who have
always believed in me.

CONTENTS

PREFACE

India is often called the 'Land of the Tiger' but it is also a country inhabited by the largest number of big cat species in the world, such as the Indian leopard, the Asiatic lion, the snow leopard, the clouded leopard and the newly translocated Asiatic cheetah. Leopards—the most adaptable big cats—inhabit a wide range of habitats: the dry deciduous forests in the Central Indian landscape, the Western ghats, the Eastern ghats, the Terai and Shivalik hills of the Himalayas, as well as the semi-arid regions of Rajasthan. Leopards are highly enigmatic and elusive in nature, able to deceive their prey to a great extent. As a result, they are regarded as one of the most powerful hunters in the wild. However, the leopards of India do not enjoy the star status of the tigers, despite being crucially important to the ecosystem.

Due to rapid urbanisation, forest cover in India has been shrinking at a brisk pace. As a result of such habitat loss and the lack of prey base, there have been several instances of leopards venturing into human settlements, leading to man–animal conflict. The Sanjay Gandhi National Park in Maharashtra is a significant example of this kind of conflict, with several incidents being reported in Mumbai over the last two decades. However, there exists a place where leopards and humans co-exist peacefully despite a densely populated location—Jhalana, a leopard conservation reserve in the Pink City of Jaipur in Rajasthan.

Jhalana, a small forested land (about 20 sq km) surrounded by the Aravallis, located in southern Jaipur, has one of the highest densities of leopards in the entire country. As per the 2022 census, there are more than 40 'urban' leopards in the entire landscape, which is quite a high number when we consider the size of the area. Before being declared as the country's first leopard conservation reserve in 2018, Jhalana used to be the hunting ground of the *maharajas* of Jaipur. Albeit small in area, Jhalana is rich in biodiversity. Apart from leopards, striped hyenas, desert foxes, chital, jungle cats, nilgai, grey langurs, jackals and sambar also live in this habitat, amongst many other species. In 2016, the Rajasthan Forest Department decided to start eco-tourism activities inside Jhalana, prior to which one had to take special permission from the Forest Department in order to enter the forest area.

Sighting leopards in the wild is not easy, especially in comparison with tiger sightings. But in Jhalana, the probability of sighting a leopard is as high as 90–95% and the animals are usually sighted in close proximity.

This book has been put together as a collection of my experiences during my field research in Jhalana in 2018, and the various challenges I faced in the process of photographing the leopards of Jhalana. I have also tried to highlight the differences between the behaviours of Jhalana's urban leopards and the leopards in the rest of the country and elaborate upon why Jhalana continues to be a safe habitat for urban leopards.

In conclusion, this book has been primarily written in order to increase awareness about leopards and other wildlife amidst urban areas, and encourage people from various demographics to unite and work towards creating thriving environments for the majestic leopards of India.

THE INDIAN LEOPARD

The evolution of the leopard

The leopard belongs to the genus *Panthera* and *pardus* is the specific epithet that differentiates it from other members of the same genus. The *Panthera* genus contains the largest living members of the cat family (tigers, lions, jaguars, leopards and snow leopards) with distinct physical characteristics that enable them to roar.

According to fossil-based evidence, the oldest ancestors of the leopard were the Miacidae, or the 'first true carnivores', that lived about 65–33.9 million years ago. These mammals were small in size but were agile tree-climbers. Scientists, however, believe the *Pseudaelurus*—a prehistoric cat that lived in Europe, Asia and North America between 20–8 million years ago—to be the direct ancestor of leopards and other big cats. As per wildlife scientists, the tiger was the first species that bifurcated from the common *Panthera* ancestors, whereas other members such as leopards, lions and jaguars evolved much later.

Species history is crucial for evolutionary research and conservation. Therefore, in order to find out the exact historic data of a particular endangered species, one has to study the DNA sequences obtained from historical samples. The leopard is an example of a large carnivore species that is currently distributed across a fraction of its historical home range. On account of habitat destruction and rapid urbanisation along with rampant poaching, leopards have become extinct from large parts of Asia. Fossil records and genetic data from modern and historical samples indicate that the leopards of Asia are closely related to their African cousins.

The oldest leopard fossils have been recovered in Eastern Africa. According to wildlife scientists, the oldest evidence of leopards in Asia was found in Pakistan, which suggests that these felids might have migrated from Africa to Asia around two million years ago.

The Javan leopard was established on the Indonesian island of Java around 375,000 years ago. On studying the morphological and genetic distinctiveness of the Javan leopard as compared to the mainland leopards of Asia, it

PREVIOUS PAGES:
The Indian leopard

ABOVE RIGHT:
The African leopard
© *Peter Githaka*

RIGHT:
The Javan leopard
© *Cloudtail the Snow Leopard/Flickr*

has been found that the Javan population can be assigned to the subspecies *Panthera pardus melas.* Hence, it can be concluded that the Javan leopard originated from the leopards of Asia. It has been suggested that that the Javan leopard represents a relict population which has descended from the Southeast Asian mainland leopard during the Middle Pleistocene period. After that, it became isolated from the Sundaic islands. The question, then, remains—how did the leopard translocate from the Southeast Asian mainland to Java? As trade routes between the Southeast Asian islands and the mainland have been reported to have existed for almost 2000 years, the leopard could have been moved to Java via human-mitigated routes, possibly through live animal trade.[1]

The current status of the Indian leopard

Although the tiger demands most of the limelight in the country, the Indian leopard (*Panthera pardus fusca*), who happens to be its close cousin, plays an equally important role in the food chain. Not unlike the tiger, these rosetted felines are also under constant threat. As per the Wildlife Institute of India's (WII) 2018 census, leopard

RIGHT: A Jawai leopard on the prowl

numbers in India roughly range from 12,000 to 14,000; however, there are several Protected Areas (PAs) which don't have an official record of the leopards thriving in nearby areas. Compared to the stringent tiger censuses conducted in the country, this lack of data on leopards is alarming. Indian leopards are listed as 'Vulnerable' in the International Union for Conservation of Nature (IUCN) Red List of Threatened Species because of habitat loss, rampant poaching and the illegal trade of skins.

Over the years, rapid urbanisation has been causing serious damage to our natural heritage. As a result, habitat loss and reduction in forest cover have become global issues which ultimately give rise to man–animal conflict. However, there are quite a few places in India where man and leopard co-exist peacefully. Jawai Bandh, located in north-western Rajasthan, often termed as India's Leopard Hill, is one place where leopards and humans have been sharing the same habitat without any conflict. Jhalana is also one such area.

Leopards are also falling victim to infrastructure development, such as highways being constructed at a rapid pace by wiping out forest patches and critical

RIGHT: A female leopard in Jhalana focuses on her target

wildlife corridors. The Nagpur to Kanha highway passes through the Kanha–Pench corridor and poses a great threat to wildlife, with many cases of leopards and tigers being run over by vehicles.

Morphological features and behaviour

Like tigers and their unique stripe patterns, every leopard possesses a different rosette pattern. These felines have smaller heads with powerful jaws and long tails. The average length of their body is 7 ft (215 cm). A large muscular male can even be as long as 8 ft. On an average, female leopards weigh up to 35 kg whereas males can weigh between 50 to 77 kg. Leopards are sexually dimorphic.

Leopards have the most varied diet of all felids. Their diet ranges from small prey species like squirrels, peacocks and wild hares to medium and larger prey like langurs, chital, nilgai, sambar, etc.

In cases where leopards live close to human settlements, they often feed upon stray dogs, goats, and livestock as well.

These felines are pretty agile and can run up to speeds of approximately 60 kph and jump as high as

LEFT: A leopard patiently waits in the Pench National Park

10 ft. With their sheer muscular strength, leopards are excellent climbers and can drag their prey up the tree to hide them from other predators. Leopards are highly unsocial; they do not like to live in packs like most other big cats. Interestingly, there is an exception in Perwa, located in the Pali (Jawai) district of Rajasthan, where leopards are frequently sighted living in a pride of 10–12 cats. However, they are mainly solitary beasts. Being highly nocturnal hunters, leopards are also opportunistic, waiting for the perfect ambush in order to deceive their prey.

The home range for male leopards spans up to 50 sq km, reducing to about 17 sq km for the females. Leopards belonging to the tropical evergreen forests of southern India and the foothills of the Himalayas like to live in trees, since they have to constantly compete with other predators like tigers and dholes. In drier areas like Rajasthan and Gujarat, they prefer to live inside caves.

When we talk about leopards, we often come across the infamous 'black panther'. However, black panthers, often mistaken as a different species, fall in the same category as any other leopard. This morphological

RIGHT: A rare pride of leopards in Jawai

characteristic that affects their coat is called 'melanism'. Nagarhole (Kabini), Mudumalai, Periyar, BRT, Dandeli, Pench and Tadoba are a few Protected Areas where melanistic leopards aka black panthers are found.

Why do leopards lick their paws?

It is quite common to see big cats like tigers, leopards or lions licking their paws. This is a way for them to clean themselves by spreading saliva all over their body, which actually helps them with grooming and cooling their body temperature. As per renowned veterinarian, Dr Pamela Perry (a resident of the Animal Behavior Clinic at Cornell University's College of Veterinary Medicine), big cats spend approximately 30% of their time grooming themselves. According to the Cummings School of Veterinary Medicine at Tufts University, another reason behind this behaviour is that it releases endorphins.

As per veterinary experts, saliva present in felines and other animals contains tissue factor which fosters the blood clotting mechanism. The lysozyme enzyme is found in many tissues and is known to attack the cell walls of many gram-positive bacteria, thus providing a defense against any infection. Salivary tissue factor,

FACING PAGE:
A Rajaji leopard in its usual roost

PG 26–27:
A Jhalana leopard licks her paws

associated with microvesicles shed from cells in the mouth, promotes wound healing through the extrinsic blood coagulation cascade.[2]

Reproduction

Leopards usually mate throughout the year. The oestrous cycle lasts for about 46 days. When in captivity, the female produces the first litter between two to four years of age. Normally, 2–3 cubs are born in a litter, occasionally going up to four. Since the cubs are under continuous threat from other predators like tigers, dholes, pythons, lions and even male leopards, mortality rates of leopard cubs are about 41–50 %. The gestation period lasts for about 87–94 days. Cubs are born with closed eyes, which usually open 4–9 days after birth. After turning three months old, the cubs tend to follow their mother in order to learn hunting skills. After they turn a year old, the cubs try to hunt by themselves, but they remain with their mother until they attain the age of two. The average life span of leopards is estimated to be 12–18 years.

LEFT: A Rajaji tigress grooms herself lavishly

Sharing space with other carnivores

As leopards inhabit a wide range of habitats, there are several places in India where they share their habitat with hyenas and wolves. Like leopards, hyenas have the ability to survive in diverse habitats; however, the same cannot be said for wolves. In India, wolves are known as the 'kings of the grassland ecosystem', since they do not thrive in other habitats. Kailadevi Wildlife Sanctuary, Saswad and Bhigwan are a few places where leopards, wolves and hyenas share the same habitat.

As per a 2019 occupancy study conducted by Wildlife Conservation Society (WCS-India) in western Maharashtra across an 89,000 sq km area, only 2500 km is assigned to Protected Areas. The study also revealed that 75% of semi-arid landscapes are occupied by hyenas, followed by Indian wolves at 64% and leopards at 57%. The study highlighted a high probability of all three species existing together across 25% of the study site.

For instance, in Pune, we find that the outskirts of the city have fragmented grassland ecosystems which are inhabited by these carnivores.

LEFT: Leopards are notoriously possessive about their cubs

Scientists, however, have emphasised on expanding the current narratives to recognise the potential of human-dominated landscapes as a conservation habitat where people and predators co-exist peacefully.

Significance of leopards in Indian culture and Hindu mythology

Animals play a significant role in tribal culture and mythology. For instance, *Waghoba* is described as a tiger/leopard deity that has been worshipped by a large number of tribes (especially by the Warli tribes of Maharashtra) in India for centuries, in order to gain protection from leopards and tigers. *Waghoba* is visualised as a large cat carved out of stone or wood and is usually painted yellow to resemble a tiger or leopard. Whether the deity is worshipped as a tiger or a leopard largely depends on regional context. In recent years, researchers have identified more than 150 shrines dedicated to worshiping *Waghoba*.[3]

ABOVE:
A traditional *Waghoba* shrine
© *V Athreya*

FACING PAGE:
A pack of Indian wolves on the outskirts of Solapur, Maharashtra

Waghoba is the combination of two Marathi words—'wagh' (tiger/leopard) and 'ba' (term of respect). A study was conducted by Wildlife Conservation Trust (WCT) and WCS on the Warli tribe to explore people's narratives on *Waghoba's* role in the lives of the Warli.

People from the Warli community shared countless stories describing how *Waghoba* (the Tiger/Leopard God) would act as the prime savior of the Warli community. Not only do the Warli tribes have an intimate familiarity with these rituals but they also possess sound knowledge regarding the behaviour of leopards.

Let's take the example of Jawai, the Leopard Hill. As discussed previously, the human–leopard conflict in Jawai is almost zero despite the fact that leopards living there usually feed on the livestock of the locals (the Rabari tribes). Man and animal have been co-existing in peace for years in this region. But who are the Rabaris and what might be the reason behind this unusual co-existence of humans and leopards? The Rabaris are a tribal caste of semi-nomadic cattle herders and shepherds who had migrated from Iran to Rajasthan, and finally to Gujarat, thousands of years ago. They worship the leopard as their sacred deity and they consider the loss of their livestock as an offering to the deity.[4]

As per a *Mongabay* report[5] from December 2019, a study was conducted in Hamirpur, a small village in Himachal Pradesh which has a decent population of

LEFT: A Maharashtrian *Waghoba* in action

leopards. In that village, leopards feeding on the livestock was nothing new. During the survey, when the researcher interviewed the locals about what they thought of a predator like the leopard inhabiting the same landscape as them, they replied, 'The leopards are not our enemy; for us, they are conscious thinking beings who can be negotiated with in order to co-exist.' The researcher also discovered that local mythology and religious beliefs play an important role in this positive attitude that the villagers of Hamirpur have towards leopards. A local myth says that Lord Shiva awarded a boon to the leopards so they can eat whatever they wish to.

In another case, a local priest told the researcher that leopards also protect human beings from being attacked by robbers while venturing deep into the forest. As the myth goes, much like dogs, leopards follow people, escorting them to their residence and if a man comes across a dacoit on the way, the leopard kills him. The leopard's status as a savior has also compelled some of Hamirpur's residents to believe that wearing leopard claws and teeth will protect them from danger.

Wildlife scientists and researchers may contradict these local myths and beliefs, but this lore plays an important role in conservation, acting as a tolerance-

ABOVE:
A Rabari elder
© *Alessandro Bergamini*

FACING PAGE:
A leopard in Sena, Jawai

building mechanism, and could help more communities learn how to share space with the leopards in their area.

Morphological differences with other leopards across India

The Indian leopard is a sleek, short-haired animal sporting a reddish-yellow coat adorned with small, close-set rosettes; however, there is considerable colour variation among the leopards of India. For instance, if we compare the leopards of central/south India, or even Jhalana, with the leopards of north-western Rajasthan (Jawai), we see that the leopards of Jawai are comparatively paler in colour.

Further differences among the leopards of India will be covered in greater detail in Chapter 4.

ABOVE:
Leopards in central India have brighter coats

FACING PAGE:
Jawai leopards are paler in colour

Endnotes:

1. Johanna L. Paijmans et al., "Historical Biogeography of the Leopard (Panthera Pardus) and Its Extinct Eurasian Populations," *BMC Evolutionary Biology* 18, no. 1 (October 23, 2018), https://doi.org/10.1186/s12862-018-1268-0.
2. Anthony J. Glazko and David M. Greenberg, "The Mechanism of the Action of Saliva in Blood Coagulation," *American Journal of Physiology-Legacy Content* 125, no. 1 (December 31, 1938): 108–12, https://doi.org/10.1152/ajplegacy.1938.125.1.108.
3. "The Warli and the Waghoba: How a Large Cat Deity Helps People to Share Space with Leopards in India," WCSNewsroom, July 8, 2021, https://newsroom.wcs.org/News-Releases/articleType/ArticleView/articleId/16351/The-Warli-and-the-Waghoba-How-a-Large-Cat-Deity-Helps-People-to-Share-Space-with-Leopards-in-India.aspx.
4. Isabella Tree, "This Indian Community Welcomes Leopards," https://www.nationalgeographic.com/, March 22, 2019, https://www.nationalgeographic.com/animals/article/leopards-coexist-hindu-community-india.
5. Aathira Perinchery, "Worshipping Waghoba: Faith Meets Conservation in Maharashtra Where Humans and Leopards Share Space," Mongabay, October 4, 2021, https://india.mongabay.com/2021/10/worshipping-waghoba-faith-meets-conservation-in-maharashtra-where-humans-and-leopards-share-space/.

THE RISE OF JHALANA

An introduction to Jhalana

Jhalana—the country's first leopard conservation reserve—is a small, fragmented forest land surrounded by the Aravalli mountains on the outskirts of southern Jaipur. It has an area of approximately 20 sq km, with a rugged, undulating terrain. At about 410–520 m above sea level, its highest point is Shikar Oudi. Jhalana is contiguous to the Amagarh Leopard Reserve, Nahargarh Wildlife Sanctuary and Jamwa Ramgarh Sanctuary, with animals often migrating between these places. Earlier, Jhalana used to be the hunting ground of the *maharajas* of this princely state. Jhalana is divided into 3 zones—Neemgatta, Lala Kund

LEFT: Jhalana Leopard Conservation Reserve

NEXT PAGE: Jhalana's high leopard density

ABOVE: Eco-tourism in Jhalana

RIGHT: A Zone 2 leopard zones in on its prey

and Toota Bandha, although work is in progress to open a few more tracks for better wildlife tracking.

Due to the presence of ample water bodies in the region, animals have access to sufficient water even in the harsh summer months. Out of these three zones, Neemgatta (Zone 1) is dense in terms of vegetation.

On the other hand, Lala Kund (Zone 2) has much less vegetation with a comparatively less undulating surface and a few ravines as well. Toota Bandha (Zone 3) comprises a hilly terrain with small ravines. On account of the undulating surface, the leopard sightings in Zone 3 are relatively fewer.

ABOVE: A female leopard in Zone 1

LEFT: A sly leopard sighting in Zone 3

FACING PAGE: A jungle gym in Zone 1

Located in the desert state of Rajasthan, Jhalana is typical example of a dry deciduous forest with rocky cliffs. The main plant species found here are thorny acacia, neem, dhok, ber, banyan, arjun, etc.

Albeit small in area, Jhalana is rich in biodiversity. Apart from the leopard, the striped hyena, desert fox, golden jackal, jungle cat, nilgai, chital, sambar and several other species inhabit this area. Jhalana is also home to a wide variety of avian species that include the red-whiskered bulbul, rufous treepie, shikra, white-eyed buzzard, common hoopoe, Asian paradise flycatcher, Indian roller, white-throated kingfisher, green bee-eater, grey francolin, Indian pitta, purple-rumped sunbird, spotted owlet, Eurasian collared dove and more.

ABOVE:
A nilgai spotting in Jhalana

FACING PAGE ABOVE:
The white-throated kingfisher

FACING PAGE BELOW:
The common hoopoe

PG 48:
The wily desert fox

PG 49:
A striped hyena in Jhalana

The Rise of Jhalana

The journey hasn't been all that easy for Jhalana. Since it is located in Malviya Nagar, a residential area in southern Jaipur, previously, people used to enter the area without any permission from the Forest Department and create a nuisance, ultimately disturbing the biodiversity on a whole. Local wildlife enthusiasts tried their level best to convert this reserve forest patch into a leopard conservation reserve in order to stop this illegal infiltration. In 2016, the Rajasthan Forest Department decided to officially open it up to the public for tourism purposes and in the following year, plans were initiated to convert Jhalana into the country's first leopard conservation reserve as part of Project Leopard. The main aim of this project was to understand and minimise man–leopard conflict and protect this magnificent creature from poaching, consequently preserving the prey–predator relationship and enhancing the prey base for these felids. The project spreads across 2000 sq km that includes sanctuaries such as the Jhalana Leopard Conservation Reserve, Kumbhalgarh Wildlife Sanctuary, Bassi Sanctuary, Jawai Bandh Leopard Conservation Reserve, Mt Abu Sanctuary, Khetri Bansyal Conservation Reserve, etc.

PG 52:
The elegant chital

PG 53:
The alert shikra

FACING PAGE:
A Jhalana leopard relaxes on an abandoned building

But the project hasn't yet expanded to other states, where there has been constant man–leopard conflict over the years. In Uttarakhand, these cases have always been significant; due to a lack of food, leopards in those areas sometimes target and kill humans, and then are either beaten to death or shot by vindictive locals.

Previously, Project Tiger and Project Rhino have been implemented in the country, but Project Leopard has been the first conservation effort of its kind in the world. This initiative has immense potential to protect these majestic felines and may become an eye-opener for other states. The leopard numbers in Jhalana have doubled from 2016 to 2022. As per the 2022 census, there are 40+ leopards inside the reserve.

Until the year 2016, the term 'urban leopard' used to be synonymous with Mumbai due to the presence of Sanjay Gandhi National Park (SGNP). Almost six times the size of Jhalana, man–animal conflict in and around SGNP continues to be an issue to this day. The Aarey Milk Colony, IIT Bombay and the National Institute of Industrial Engineering are all contiguous to SGNP. Leopards often enter these areas, which is a cause for

RIGHT: Jhalana, a fully fenced reserve

concern. However, it is important to remember that animals don't recognise man-made boundaries. Weaker leopards are pushed out of the park by the stronger ones, ultimately causing them to enter residential areas and provoke man–animal conflict. In contrast, Jhalana has a limited area of 20–25 sq km but despite leopard numbers having multiplied over the last few years, the human–leopard conflict has been close to negligible here.

Jhalana's biggest advantage is that it is the only Protected Area in India which has been fully fenced. Due to the growing leopard population in Jhalana, there has been a slight rise in recent incidents with leopards entering residential areas in Malviya Nagar, but they have been navigated efficiently by the authorities. Another advantage is that Jhalana is well-connected with the newly formed Amagarh Leopard Reserve and the Nahargarh Wildlife Sanctuary, forming a wildlife corridor. Leopards commonly migrate between Amagarh, Jhalana and Nahargarh, thus maintaining a demographic balance in each area and ensuring that the weaker leopards don't venture out of the reserves into

RIGHT: A leopard roams around freely in Jhalana

human settlements. Chapter 1 explains how the leopards of Jawai have adapted to live peacefully with the locals. It seems that the leopards of Jhalana have taken a cue from their counterparts in Jawai and are setting an example of how man and leopard can co-exist peacefully.

Before Jhalana came into the limelight, wildlife enthusiasts and photographers used to spend a considerable amount of money to visit Kabini, Bandipur, Panna, Satpura, Jawai, etc. in order to photograph a leopard in the wild. With the rise of Jhalana, tourists seem to have found an alternative. Since Jhalana's safari tariff is much lower as compared to the aforementioned places, photographers from India as well as abroad throng to Jhalana in large numbers. In the current landscape, it wouldn't be an exaggeration to say that Jhalana is the best place in the country to spot an urban leopard in its full glory.

Understanding the dietary patterns of the leopards of Jhalana

Being highly adaptable, leopards are the only big cats which live near rural as well as urban settlements. For

RIGHT: A quick jaunt to the watering hole

this reason, their diet spans a wide range of species, from stray dogs and livestock to wild animals like deer, antelope, etc. Their diet differs from place to place. For example, the leopards of Rajasthan have different feeding patterns as compared to the leopards of south and central India.

In order to protect this felid species, it is very important to understand their feeding patterns, as efforts to conserve their prey will in turn serve to protect these predators. There has been significant research work conducted in India regarding the dietary patterns of leopards in various regions. However, until my study in 2018, there hadn't been any substantial research work done in Jhalana. Astonishingly, this place remains relatively unknown to locals in Jaipur and nearby places. Therefore, the chance to conduct research in this newly formed leopard reserve was a significant opportunity for me.

Over the last few years, Jhalana has cruised way ahead of other prominent leopard reserves in India like the Jawai Bandh reserve, due to extraordinary leopard sightings in recent times owing to its high leopard density.

RIGHT: Female leopards scout for smaller prey

After procuring permission from the Rajasthan Forest Department, I commenced my research work on identifying the dietary patterns of leopards in Jhalana in May 2018. Ideally, winter is considered the best time for commencing field work because the weather is much more pleasant as compared to the summer months when the temperature rises above 46°C in the day. Nonetheless, I took on the challenge and started my research.

My findings revealed that in Jhalana, the dietary patterns of leopards vary with age and sex, with the female leopards targeting mostly small and medium prey species like the grey langur and rhesus macaque, while the males prey on larger species like the nilgai and spotted deer.

On the contrary, the dietary patterns of male and female leopards in other reserves in the country are almost the same. When it comes to age, sub-adult leopards of both sexes in Jhalana target smaller prey like peacocks, rabbits and fowl whereas older males target larger prey, as mentioned above.

LEFT: A male leopard feeding on nilgai in Jhalana

Meet the Leopards of Jhalana

Let's take a look at some of the famous leopards of Jhalana I was able to capture on my lens during my frequent visits to the reserve.

Flora

Flora is the current queen of Jhalana and has birthed the maximum number of cubs. She can usually be seen in both Zone 1 & 2.

Juliet

Juliet was a female leopard born to Flora; she was one of the boldest leopards I have ever met. Juliet was last seen in 2019, after which she left the tourism zone and is presumed to have passed away since.

Cleopatra

Cleopatra was part of Flora's litter. Unlike her sister Juliet, she was a bit shy in her approach and wasn't very friendly with tourists. As per the most recent update, she has moved to the Amagarh Leopard Reserve adjoining Jhalana.

LEFT: Meet Flora, the Queen of Jhalana

PG 68: Juliet eyes the camera from a distance

PG 69: Cleopatra with her hypnotic gaze

Simba

Simba, a young male, was born to Flora in 2019. He is currently the reigning prince of Jhalana and has made Zone 3 his territory. Earlier, he was usually seen in Zone 1 and 2 but in the year 2020, Simba had a massive fight with another male, Rana, which compelled him to move to Zone 3.

Prince

Prince belonged to Flora's first litter. In 2016, Prince became the blue-eyed boy of Jhalana. He was bold and aggressive, yet very tourist-friendly, hardly bothered by their presence. After an injury back in 2019, Prince moved out of Jhalana. He is currently in the Amagarh Leopard Reserve.

Rana

Born to Mrs Khan, Rana rose to stardom in 2020 after a massive fight with Simba. Eventually, he won the fight and currently, he has made both Zone 1 & 2 his territory.

LEFT: Simba surveils his territory
PG 72: Prince awaits his next kill
PG 73: Rana in a thoughtful moment

Kesar

Kesar was a male leopard born to Flora. Unfortunately, he ventured out of the park around 2021–22 and eventually died after an accident.

Mrs Khan

Mrs Khan was born to Boodhi Amma in the mining area of Jhalana. 'Khan' is the Hindi word for 'mine', hence the name. Second to only Flora, Mrs Khan has given birth to the highest number of cubs in the area. Currently, she resides in the mining area along with her daughter.

LEFT: The late Kesar

PG 76: Mrs Khan caught mid-leap

PG 77: The camera stares back at Mrs Khan

A JOURNEY THROUGH JHALANA

Budding friendships

I was perhaps one of the first photographers to explore Jhalana, which is why I have been able to document some of the most well-known leopards of the region. In 2016, Jhalana was all about Flora, the erstwhile queen, before her daughter, Juliet, stole the limelight in 2018, carrying her mother's legacy forward. Juliet was possibly the most daring female I had ever seen in Jhalana. She had one sister, Cleopatra, who was quite timid in her approach, and not as tourist-friendly as her sister. When I was doing my research work in Jhalana in 2018 and closely observing Juliet, I was baffled by her boldness. Practically every time I entered the park premise, I was

LEFT: The spunky Juliet

greeted by her. It almost felt as if she was getting used to me. When Juliet was in the tourism zone, she would never let any other female leopard settle down in her area, except for her mother and sister. Although I am aware that it takes years to understand the ecology of big cats, after having followed Juliet for a substantial amount of time, I can say that I was able to grasp her movement patterns to some extent. Leopards are inscrutable big cats, much shyer than tigers and lions, but if you can manage to win their trust and they sense that you are not a threat, the leopard will most likely connect with you.

I am privileged to have experienced this connection with Juliet. An incident that highlighted this bond occurred in July 2018, when I was on an evening drive. The atmosphere was placid, the muddy track fenced on both sides with scrubby vegetation. I encountered Flora at around 5 pm. She was trying to cross the road.

Flora appeared to be pregnant during that period. After she had finally moved back into the thicket, everyone was elated about having seen her at such close quarters. Most people decided to leave as it was getting dark, even though there were still 15 minutes left for the park to close its gates. It is said that when you are on a safari, it's always best to wait till the very last moment before leaving, since

ABOVE:
Juliet on a casual evening stroll

PG 82–83:
Flora crossing the road confidentally

a lot can happen in the five minutes before the park closes. So I decided to stay back. After a few minutes, I heard an urgent alarm call from the langurs nearby. As I was trying to figure out if it was Juliet or some other leopard I knew, my driver suddenly pointed out some movement in the thicket nearby. It *was* Juliet! She was trying to remain secluded, and later on, we found out that she had made a recent kill, which explained the seclusion. She came out of hiding for a brief moment before disappearing into the dark. Since the other jeeps had already left the park, I was the only one who was present and who was blessed enough to get a chance to photograph Juliet. I'd personally like to believe that she wouldn't have come out of the bushes had it been someone else in my place!

RJ14TD8800

Back with a vengeance

Though Jhalana remains open throughout the year, I usually prefer to visit in the monsoon period because a majority of the other Protected Areas are closed due to heavy rain during this season, and the jungle turns lush green, providing the perfect contrast for leopard photographs. But with COVID-19 halting my plans in 2020, I couldn't make it to Jhalana in the monsoon and decided to go during winter instead. It was early December; although the usual northern cold wave hadn't started yet, the mornings were still a bit chilly. Since my previous safari hadn't been that successful, I was hoping to get some good pictures on my upcoming morning drive. Excited, we entered the park premises bright and early at 6 am. It was quite cold and the forest was engulfed with a thick blanket of haze, as we had expected.

At first, we spotted chattering common babblers along with grey francolins. A herd of nilgai were grazing in a grassy patch and a couple of grey langurs were munching on fruit in the trees above. After roaming around for about an hour without any success, we decided to take a different route and ultimately reached Zone 2. As soon as we entered, we saw the fresh pugmarks of a leopard. We moved farther ahead to investigate and saw a queue of jeeps standing near a watering hole (locally called the 'Illegal Waterhole'). While talking to the other tourists, we discovered that a leopard had been seen moving towards the Illegal Waterhole. But since the surrounding foliage was quite dense, the leopard might have hidden somewhere secluded. Thus, we decided to wait there for a while in the hope of photographing the leopard. After about 20 minutes, suddenly, we heard a strong alarm call by nilgai nearby. We promptly decided to move towards the place where the alarm call was sounded. Within a split second, I noticed some movement amidst the bushes and was finally able to spot the leopard.

It was the reigning Prince of Jhalana—Simba! Although he was initially trying his best to remain secluded, he finally emerged from the bushes and attempted to ambush the nilgai. Later on, he changed his mind and slowly moved towards the watering hole in order to quench his thirst. What a sight that was for a photographer! Born to Flora (Queen of Jhalana), Simba was young but bold, following his mother's legacy.

Simba was not disturbed by our presence, spending about 15 minutes at the watering hole before vanishing into the dense canopy. With a few exceptions, the leopards residing in Jhalana are quite bold and

PG 84:
Juliet peeks through the bushes

PG 85:
A pregnant Flora

PG 88:
Simba hiding in the thicket

PG 89:
In search of a watering hole

S.P. 1728

tourist-friendly, which is the most striking feature of this small forested land amidst the busy city of Jaipur. This particular sighting was in such close proximity that it was quite a challenge for photographers using the 600 mm lens.

Simba was such a dominant young male that he made his presence felt every time I visited Jhalana. He used to be majorly sighted in Zone 2, but in the year 2021, he was challenged by another young male, Rana, and there was a massive fight between the two animals. Eventually, Simba lost the battle and was forced to leave his territory in Zone 2. The locals say that after 2021, Simba went on to settle down in Zone 3 where his sightings are not as frequent. One day, perhaps, he might return with a vengeance and take back his original territory.

Boldness at its best

In the early monsoon of 2021, I was on my first afternoon safari in Jhalana. The weather was pleasant with overcast conditions, but I was slightly skeptical, as a sudden passing shower could ruin my entire safari.

Trying to stay optimistic, we entered Zone 2 and were in the process of tracking down a female leopard

PG 90–91: The predator and the prey

LEFT: Simba quenches his thirst

that was sighted the previous evening. Since it was a weekday, Jhalana was completely devoid of local crowds and other tourists. Consequently, I was quite happy to be able to enjoy the serenity inside the park.

Our driver cum naturalist had been leaning over the door of the vehicle for a while, examining a large set of pugmarks and muttering under his breath. It seemed that a female leopard might have crossed the road a few minutes earlier. Our naturalist decided to wait for a while. After about 15 minutes, we decided to move ahead and entered Zone 1. As soon as we were there, we were informed that Flora had been sighted by some jeeps a little while ago, but our naturalist thought that we should keep an eye out for other leopards as well. Hence, we started moving towards the mining area. Another jeep approaching from the other side signalled us to move quickly. Our driver picked up the speed and reached the mining area right away. I saw a queue of 4–5 jeeps standing near the watchtower. Without wasting any time, I asked one of them what was going on and was informed that a male leopard was resting atop the watchtower. Our driver jumped to it and promptly entered the watchtower from the back.

FACING PAGE:
Rana taking a moment to unwind

From this angle, the leopard was clearly visible and I was told that this was Rana. I was completely mesmerised

by his beauty and boldness. He seemed to be resting after a heavy meal. Since there were only 4–5 jeeps, I didn't have much trouble capturing the moment. And what a moment it was! Rana was in his prime. His coat was neither yellow, nor orange, but a true buttery gold, like silk lit up from within. Most forests are full of surprises and beautiful, occasionally transcendent moments. But there is nothing that can beat the sighting of a leopard perched on an abandoned watchtower. Rana was so comfortable in his resting position that he only lifted his head a few times when the other jeeps reached the watch tower, not bothering to leave his majestic perch. The thrill of photographing this urban leopard in his makeshift lair was remarkable.

This series of images demonstrates the boldness of this young male leopard. One thing I must say, though, is that Rana wasn't as bold when he was first sighted in the tourist-designated area. It is possible that the battle with Simba changed his approach significantly.

Expect the unexpected

The next time I visited Jhalana was in August 2022, and this time, I was accompanied by one of my batchmates.

LEFT: Following Mrs Khan and her daughter

Since our first morning safari on that visit was completely ruined by heavy rain, we were hoping that the sun would come out and rescue our next safari. Although Jhalana as a location practically guarantees you a leopard sighting, one can never predict the weather.

It was a quarter to three when our jeep arrived to collect us. Although overcast conditions were still prevailing, the weather was much better than the morning. As we were accompanied by an expert tracker, I was hoping for a good sighting.

Since Zone 2 was completely silent in terms of animal activity, our naturalist decided to move into Zone 1. As we headed towards Neemgatta, the muddy track was fringed on both sides by the scrubby forest and the air aged like fine wine, getting purer as we went deeper into the forest.

After driving around for half an hour, we finally went towards Khan, the mining area. As soon as we climbed up the ridge, we saw a pair of leopards walking about quietly—it was Mrs Khan and her daughter. My driver promptly switched off the engine and began to slowly follow the leopards. I was completely hypnotised by this

RIGHT: Mrs Khan sees us following her

unexpected encounter. Since we were the only ones out there, we were in no hurry to photograph the leopards, choosing to merely follow them cautiously. Suddenly, one of them turned around and spotted us.

In an instant, she disappeared into the thicket. Meanwhile, we moved farther ahead and hid underneath a dhok tree. My naturalist seemed quite confident, promising me the chance to get a proper headshot of the leopards. After waiting there patiently for about 10 minutes, the mother–daughter duo finally appeared right in front of us. It seemed like Mrs Khan and her daughter were totally unaware of our presence, which made for the perfect shooting opportunity.

She did spot us later on, but this time, she was bolder. It seemed as if Mrs Khan and her daughter weren't bothered by us anymore. The duo sat down on the road for a moment before going back into seclusion. By then, I had already taken a substantial number of pictures. What a wonderful encounter! This was perhaps the first time I was able to capture two leopards in one frame inside Jhalana, since this kind of sighting is extremely rare.

LEFT: The mother–daughter duo retreats

PG 102–103: Mother and daughter sticking together through thick and thin

LEOPARDS OF INDIA: A COMPARATIVE STUDY

Leopards of Central India

After completing my research on the leopards of Jhalana in 2018, I decided to explore other Protected Areas with high leopard densities. My mission was not limited to merely photographing other leopards; I also tried to develop an understanding of how their behavioural approach differs from Jhalana's leopards.

To begin this journey, I first targeted the Panna Tiger Reserve (PTR) which has quite a healthy leopard population. Way back in 2009, when the entire tiger population of PTR was completely eliminated on account of rampant poaching, leopards became the major predator of the entire landscape. As a result of zero competition from tigers, there was a significant hike in the number of

LEFT: A leopard in the Panna Reserve

Dhundwa, the highest point in Panna

leopards. Even after the reintroduction of tigers in Panna back in 2012–13, leopard numbers still remained healthy.

I visited Panna in June 2019. Since it was a Wednesday, I knew that the park would remain closed for the second half. I asked my naturalist about sighting updates, and he told me that morning safaris had been very successful throughout the entire season. The excitement started to build for my first safari the next morning.

The rugged Ken River

The next day, we started our safari at 6.30 am. Although this was during the peak of summer, the weather was really pleasant. It was decided that we would move up the gorge—the highest point in Panna, Dhundwa—where a female leopard was sighted the previous evening. As soon as we reached the forest *chowki* just beneath the gorge, we heard strong alarm calls from chital. In the meantime, the forest guard also informed us that Tigress P-151 had come out into the open area near Dhundwa. Without wasting a single moment, we proceeded in the direction of the alarm call. We had hardly travelled half a kilometre, when my naturalist suddenly spotted a leopard trying to cross the road. My shutter lens instantly went into a frenzy, trying to capture this magnificent leopard. The sighting lasted for hardly 10 minutes, but that was more than enough to get some good shots. It seemed to be a bold female leopard who was barely bothered by our presence, crossing the muddy track before going back inside the thicket. This particular moment completely changed my perception regarding the behavioural approach of leopards which were not urban.

Earlier, I used to believe that only Jhalana's leopards were tourist-friendly, but I was proven wrong in Panna. After this successful expedition, I felt more encouraged to explore other places with high leopard densities and document a diverse range of leopards.

Right after visiting Panna, I made up my mind to visit the Pench Tiger Reserve in Madhya Pradesh. Although I had already visited Pench in 2015–16, I hadn't managed to spot any leopards. This time, however, the scenario had changed, since leopard sightings had been

FACING PAGE:
A Pench leopard blocks the road in style

on an all-time high at Pench in that period. In December 2019, I flew down to Nagpur on an early-morning flight, accompanied by two friends.

Since the journey from Nagpur to Pench only takes two hours, we were able to make it for the 3 pm safari. I asked my driver about the probability of spotting a leopard, upon which he assured me of a 99% chance of a sighting. I was dying to catch a glimpse of the rosetted feline. Moreover, I was equally pumped to catch a tiger on my lens since tiger sightings had been impressive during that season. Just when I was dozing off, one of my friends yelled, 'Leopard! Leopard!' I jolted awake and saw a female leopard sitting right in front of our jeep. I was completely spellbound, unsure if it was a hallucination or a real live leopard before my eyes. It took me a minute to digest the truth. Finally, I managed to gather my thoughts and took a series of photographs in rapid succession. The leopard was in such close proximity that I was having trouble framing the animal on my macro lens. Nonetheless, I was able to get some impressive shots. The sighting lasted for almost 40 minutes. We were the ones who spotted this leopard first, and more jeeps from other parts of the park arrived there later.

I was astonished by the boldness of the female leopard. In spite of being surrounded by so many jeeps, she never even moved an inch. It was a first-of-its-kind experience for me—a female leopard sitting right in front of our vehicle and casually blocking the road.

In a previous conversation with a wildlife researcher, I had discovered that the leopards of Uttarakhand and the Terai Belt of Uttar Pradesh are very aggressive. However, back-to-back sightings in Panna and Pench made me realise that the leopards of central India are equally bold (if not as aggressive) as compared to Terai leopards, while Jhalana's leopards are quite docile in contrast and have a different behavioural approach.

Only one Jhalana leopard comes to my mind when we talk about boldness, and that is the late Juliet, who has been discussed in detail in Chapter 3. Coming back to the Pench safari, the female leopard finally got up after half an hour and started moving in the opposite direction. She seemed to be in no hurry. Quite a few jeeps got a head-on shot of this leopard and the light was perfect—neither harsh nor dull. After walking down the track for 15 minutes, she changed her path and moved into the thicket.

All in all, it was a wonderful day, courtesy of our brilliant sighting of the female leopard. I will always

Dappled sunlight turning leopard coats into buttered gold

remember this as one of my best sightings outside Jhalana (probably the very best in the central Indian landscape), even if we didn't get to see any other leopards on our remaining safaris.

Apart from Panna and Pench, I also sighted leopards in Satpura and Nagzira. Although my leopard sighting at Nagzira wasn't that memorable, the sighting at Satpura deserves a special mention.

I had visited Satpura much before Jhalana and it was the first tiger reserve I had explored in central India. Unlike Kanha, Bandhavgarh and Pench, Satpura isn't that popular among wildlife enthusiasts, although there has been a growth spurt in the footfall on account of impressive tiger sightings from 2022 onwards.

2017 was my second time in Satpura, and tiger sightings were quite rare in that period. In fact, Satpura has never been projected as one of the chief tiger reserves in the country by the Madhya Pradesh Govt. On the contrary, Satpura has always been rather famous for its leopard and sloth bear sightings. It is always said that if you are in Satpura, there is a 90% chance that you will get to see leopards along with the sloth bears and this was the primary reason behind my second visit to this place. Back in 2011, I hadn't stayed at Satpura, but had come all the way from Pachmarhi and gone back right after my evening safari. The lack of information regarding the safaris at the Satpura Tiger Reserve along with the state of accommodation there compelled me to travel to and from Pachmarhi. However, after a gap of six years, things had changed drastically by 2017 and Satpura now boasted of a decent number of resorts and hotels. I stayed at Bison Resort, Madhai (a property run by the state government).

It was midsummer and the weather was unbearably hot. It was a Wednesday when I reached Satpura, a weekly off for all the tiger reserves of Madhya Pradesh. Making use of the spare time, I booked three safaris online, starting from the next evening. Later in the day,

the hotel manager informed me that he could arrange a tiger sighting for the next day. After enquiring further, I found out that a tigress along with her cubs had made a kill in the Parsapani range of Satpura, which was a buffer zone.* Without a second thought, I said yes to the offer.

Sunrise at the Satpura Tiger Reserve

* A tiger reserve/National Park is divided into 2 zones: 1. Core zone (In core zones, no human activities are allowed except strictly regulated tourism, since these areas are highly sensitive in terms of animal movement) 2. Buffer zone (human activities are allowed here to some extent)

Sloth bear sighting at Parsapani (Satpura)

The next morning, we entered the buffer zone at 6.30 am. Since the spot where the carcass was lying was at some distance, we drove at a rapid pace. Soon, we were greeted by a pair of sloth bears. The pair crossed the road and went into the thicket. Since my mind was largely occupied by the tigress, I wasn't expecting to spot a different animal at the very beginning. Nevertheless, the sight of a sloth bear with her cub in the middle of the road

First glimpse of the regal lady of Satpura

was remarkable. After a brief pause, we proceeded further and within 20 minutes, we had arrived at our destination. We saw a few jeeps already waiting there for the tigress to come out in the open. The atmosphere was completely serene; no movements, not a single alarm call. Though the stink of rotten carcass was quite present, we were unable to actually see the kill. Perhaps the tigress had hidden the carcass in a safer place in order to safeguard it against the scavengers. After waiting there for about half an hour, we were beginning to lose hope. Hence, our driver decided to take a different route. This route was quite undulating and had a very steep incline. Our driver was clearly very skilled, as navigating such tricky climbs is not a cakewalk. We had hardly been moving for a minute or so when lo and behold, there she was—the tigress, hiding in a bush nearby! I urged the driver to stop immediately; she was hardly 10 ft away.

My heart throbbed with excitement. I could barely believe my eyes at the sight of the graceful lady. I knew this was a once-in-a-lifetime moment because it is not easy to get this kind of a portrait shot of a tiger in Satpura. At that point of time, I was probably one of the very few who had been able to photograph a tiger in Satpura. This is what you call destiny, perhaps. You come here to photograph leopards and in return, are greeted with the brilliant sighting of a tiger, that too in a buffer zone. Isn't it amazing how things work out sometimes? After photographing this tigress, we went in search of her sub-adult cubs, and once again, I was lucky enough to sight them. I did get a few shots, but the images weren't up to the mark. However, I saw all of them with my own eyes and it was an unforgettable morning.

Moving on to my three upcoming safaris in the core zone—the leopard era was up next!

The next morning, we entered our safari zone by 6.30 am. It was my second safari in the core zone. Since my first safari at Madhai had been totally dry, I instructed my driver to focus strictly on the leopards, and nothing else. Consequently, we took a different route as compared to the other jeeps. The slight drizzle of the previous night had left the weather quite pleasant. Our route was not as hilly and had better visibility. As compared to other parks in central India, gaur sightings in Satpura are very high; perhaps even higher than Kanha. Due to their high population density, the gaur seemed to be grazing in almost every nook and cranny of the park. After about an hour, it seemed like the entire forest had gone into hibernation. No signs of alarm calls or pugmarks made the atmosphere inside the forest rather dull. To his credit, our driver was trying his level best to ensure that we caught at least a glimpse of a leopard. After asking the other drivers, we found out that they hadn't had any luck as well. Perhaps the previous night's rain was the spoilsport. There are no guarantees in the wild, after all.

After moving around for three hours straight without catching a break, we finally heard the first alarm call at a

FACING PAGE:
The mesmerising Queen of Satpura

quarter to ten. It was the urgent chattering of a few langurs, coming from a nearby water body. So there was still hope! As they say, never lose your patience when in the jungle, because each and every second is vital. We decided that the best thing we could do was to wait at a point where the other side of the water body would be visible. The alarm call became more prominent and within the next minute, the leopard came out of hiding. It appeared to be a large male. Although I couldn't take a picture of him, as the sighting lasted for barely 10 seconds, I was still delighted to have sighted a leopard at Satpura for the very first time (with another safari still to go!).

Now for the climax—my final safari at Satpura. It was a really hot afternoon, and we were walking down to the Madhai Boating Point after lunch. When on safari in Madhai, one has to first cross the Denwa backwaters via boat and then board their respective jeeps on the other side of the river bank. After having seen a leopard for those glorious few seconds in the morning, my adrenaline rush was at its peak. As we were moving ahead, signs of leopards seemed to be everywhere, from pugmarks to scat. Compared to my morning safari, there seemed to have been a drastic change inside the forest; the air was buzzing with energy. Even if I hadn't yet sighted a leopard, I felt as if the animal could be lurking around every other bend. After 20 minutes, we reached a place where a few jeeps were already standing in a queue. On enquiring, we discovered that one of the jeeps had sighted a leopard.

A group of langurs sitting on a nearby tree were continuously giving the alarm call. It seemed as if the leopard was on the move. After waiting for a little while, I finally saw the first glimpse of the leopard. Not just one, but *two* different leopards. Although I was finding it hard to get a full view of the leopards since I had to balance on the roof of the jeep, I was in a complete state of euphoria in that moment. Even if I wasn't able to take photographs that met my expectations, I reminded myself that the game was not over yet.

In search of better pictures, we went in a different direction. I didn't protest, as I had full faith in my driver's approach. With supreme aplomb, my driver asked me to get my camera ready, and started driving as fast as he could. I noticed that we were the only ones to have left that particular place, almost as if our driver knew exactly where those leopards would head to. We reached our destination within five minutes, at around 6.30 pm. Although the light had faded to a great extent, I

ABOVE:
The couple caught in a moment of contemplation

FACING PAGE:
The rare sight of mating leopards

knew that late evening has always been considered as the best time to see these rosetted felines. After 10 minutes, my driver whispered, 'The leopards have arrived.'

It was the large male, sitting in a meadow, hardly 30 ft away from our vehicle. After a few seconds, his partner quietly came in, and they started mating. Frozen in excitement, I completely forgot to shoot for the first few seconds, before finally managing to capture some

decent images. Irrespective of the photographs I had taken, I was astonished at the boldness of these leopards, who were busy mating, unbothered by our presence. In my experience, I had never seen leopards mating in such close proximity to human presence. All the images I had seen of mating sequences between leopards in Jhalana or Jawai had been shot from a distance, using the 600–800 mm lens. The behaviour I was currently witnessing in Satpura was quite simply out of the world, clearly showing the contrast between the leopards of central India and the urban leopards of Jhalana.

Leopards of Northwest India

Rajasthan is well-known for its robust population of leopards. As per the most recent census by the National Tiger Conservation Authority of India, the number of leopards in Rajasthan has surged from 476 in 2018 to 721 in 2022. Jawai Bandh, Kumbhalgarh, Bassi and Ranakpur are a few places with high leopard density. Although the Jawai Bandh Leopard Conservation Reserve is the most popular destination among wildlife enthusiasts, I would like to highlight Ranakpur, which is comparatively less explored as compared to Jawai, but has a very high rate of leopard sightings.

The hilly Ranakpur landscape

I usually target places which are less commercial, yet rich in biodiversity, which is why I decided to visit Ranakpur. Ranakpur has always been famous for its marble Jain temples. But of late, Ranakpur has been slowly climbing up the ladder towards becoming a wildlifer's paradise, thanks to its impressive leopard sightings.

In 2018, after coming across some striking leopard photographs from Ranakpur which inspired me to explore this uncharted place, I gradually started gathering information about the area by conversing frequently with the local naturalists. In August 2023, I finally went to Ranakpur.

Ranakpur's biggest USP lies in the fact that it is less crowded as compared to Jawai, which means that booking a safari at the last moment is quite manageable. Keeping this in my mind, I booked my safaris just a week prior to my visit.

Ranakpur is situated in the Pali district of Rajasthan, 720 km from Delhi. I started my journey at around 5 am and comfortably reached my destination by 4.30 pm.

Usually, I arrange for 4–5 safaris, but since it was monsoon and sightings were fluctuating during the mornings, I decided to skip the morning safaris and only arranged for two evening drives.

The next day, I met my naturalist at around 4.30 pm. It was quite a pleasant day, with the clouds playing hide-and-seek with the sun, and the occasional light drizzle. As we moved ahead, I was reminded of Jawai.

Like Jawai, Ranakpur's topography is also a mix of semi-arid farmlands and the rocky Aravallis. The mountains are gigantic granite hills that were formed due to volcanic eruptions years ago, and they hold a large

Ranakpur, an unexplored leopard haven

number of caves that are inhabited by leopards, hyenas, sloth bears, etc.

In Jawai, naturalists target one hill at a time, depending on the sightings, but in Ranakpur, the situation is slightly different. Here, since almost every hill is occupied by leopards, each and every hill needs to be scanned simultaneously. You never know where a leopard will pop out from. This is why you have to be around a skilled naturalist to spot the rosetted felines. The terrain we were on was a mix of farmlands and tar roads. At times, we had to climb up the hillocks and only a skilled driver can negotiate with this kind of a steep granite terrain. While my naturalist was continuously in touch with the locals regarding leopard sightings, nothing seemed to be going our way. After trying for three and a half hours, I decided to go back. My naturalist tried his best to persuade me to stay a little longer, but I had given up by then, and returned to the resort. I couldn't help but wonder what had obstructed the sighting, considering that the weather and crowd conditions seemed ideal.

The next evening, I started out slightly late, at around 5 pm. My naturalist was elated to inform me that a few

A leopard hill in Ranakpur

Parallels with the Jawai hills

locals had sighted a pair of leopards—a mother with her sub-adult male cub—at around 11 am, and there was a 90% chance that we would be able to track them down. Hence, without much thought, we moved to the place where the pair was sighted right away. It was a giant hillock with multiple caves, and the pair was inhabiting one particular cave. Usually, late evenings are considered to be the best time for a leopard sighting

A large, bold Ranakpur male eyes the horizon

but in Ranakpur, there is no certainty when a sighting will happen—mid-day or afternoon sightings are not uncommon. While scanning the hill, my naturalist decided to move to the top to get a better view of the surrounding hills.

Although the climb was really steep, and a little scary, the view from the top was amazing. After reaching the topmost point, I had a clear view of the surrounding hills and nearby caves through my binoculars. Suddenly, my

An almost-pink leopard, only spoted in Ranakpur

naturalist spotted a male leopard resting inside a cave on a nearby hill. We promptly headed there, excited. As soon as we reached there, we were disappointed to see that the leopard had left that place. It was very disheartening. But the game was not over yet. We were just about to leave the place, when suddenly, my naturalist got a call from a nearby local who had sighted a big male leopard on a cliff. We immediately headed to that spot, which was barely five minutes away.

After we arrived there, I finally spotted the elusive leopard. He was bold and large, not really bothered by human presence. Perhaps wanting to feast on a recent kill, he gave us barely 30 seconds before moving into a hideout, but that was more than enough time for me to take a few good photographs. I was grateful for the locals' thorough knowledge.

We stayed there for few more minutes, but he didn't come back. Hence, we decided to move to the hill where we had missed the earlier leopard. This time, we were lucky enough to sight that leopard as well. This one also seemed to be a big male. Interestingly, Ranakpur is the only place in India where the 'pink' leopard is found.

Though sightings of this 'pink' leopard are rare, the leopard we sighted did have a pinkish coat on his body.

What a joy it was to capture this melanistic leopard on my lens! His pinkish-yellow coat against the lush green surroundings added striking depth to my image; this is probably one of the best habitat shots I have ever captured. Although the leopard was elusive at first, I'm grateful to have finally managed to locate him. The sighting lasted for a solid five minutes before he went back into the thicket. After this, we drove back to the place where we had sighted the first large male. As soon as we reached there, we found

The majestic Ranakpur male surveys the lay of the land

him sitting on a rock. It was almost as if he was keeping an eye on his kingdom from a vantage point.

Perhaps he was trying to find prey. I was mesmerised by his charm and confidence. Through the zoom lens, it appeared to me as if a swarm of flies swirling around his forehead was agitating him. He yawned several times in order to get rid of the flies. I spent a solid 30 minutes with this gentle lad before it got totally dark.

This incident demonstrates a drastic contrast between the males in Jhalana and the rest of India. In Jhalana, the males don't usually give you a substantial amount of time to take a shot. Even if I compare Ranakpur with Jawai, which has a similar landscape, the former still has an edge. Moreover, as I recently found out, it is also one of the very few places which has a high density of male leopards. I truly believe that Ranakpur is an uncharted leopard's paradise.

Leopards of Northern India (Uttarakhand)

The leopards of Uttarakhand have always been in the news since Jim Corbett's time. Even beyond incidents involving man-eaters, there is a reason why Uttarakhand's leopards steal the limelight—the Rajaji Tiger Reserve. Since 2022, Rajaji has been boasting of some extraordinary leopard sightings, which wasn't the case even a few years ago. Corbett was always the first choice for wildlife enthusiasts. But things are changing, and photographers across India have been thronging to Rajaji to get a glimpse of these majestic Terai leopards. The main safari entrance leading to the Mohand range is situated approximately 50 km from the capital city of Dehradun. It is the newest and the most dynamic section of the Rajaji Tiger Reserve.

FACING PAGE:
Yawning keeps the flies away

I have been a regular visitor to Rajaji since 1999. Usually, I used to explore the Chilla range which is closer to Haridwar. Mainly famous for its wild elephant sightings, Chilla is never on the priority list of big cat lovers since leopard sightings are usually minimal. During that time, hardly anyone knew about the Mohand range, but things have entirely turned around now. Since 2022, the Mohand range of Rajaji has become a hotspot for leopard lovers and I finally planned my visit to this uncharted part of Rajaji in April 2023.

Before planning my Rajaji visit, I kept an eye on daily sighting updates and my findings were incredible. Not a single safari was going dry. 3–4 different leopards were being sighted daily. I wanted to make full use of this opportunity and booked four consecutive safaris. In the past, I had photographed leopards in the central Indian landscape and Rajasthan but hadn't been fortunate enough to capture one in the Terai belt of the Himalayas. According to wildlife experts, the leopards of Uttarakhand are quite bold and aggressive. Getting a chance to photograph these leopards was like a dream come true for me.

Although it was April, the weather was pleasant due to a recent bout of unseasonal rain. In all my

FACING PAGE:
Rajaji Tiger Reserve

safaris there, I was accompanied by my safari mentor, Mr Gurinderjeet Singh. Mr Singh is the man behind the newfound popularity of the Mohand range. He has been continuously tracking the leopards of the area for the last few years and has photographed 35 different leopards in the Mohand range. According to him, Mohand has evolved into a breeding ground for leopards and the main reason is the abundance of prey and a lack of competition from its larger cousin, the tiger.

Soon, we started for our evening safari and made our way to the entrance. Like everyone else, I was also hoping to catch a glimpse of a leopard right away. Compared to the Chilla range, Mohand is less undulating and a tar road covers a substantial part of this range. I asked Mr Singh what the reason for the Mohand range getting closed down during the monsoon could be. The topography there is not all that hilly and resembles the Dhela range of the Corbett National Park, which remains open throughout the year. He told me that the tar road we were on passes through 4–5 river beds which get flooded during the monsoon and ultimately obstruct vehicle movement.

Since it was my first time venturing into this part of Rajaji, I was stunned. The sky was a crystal-clear blue, like a Robin's egg. The combination of tall sal trees and yellow grass made the entire landscape remarkable. This forest patch is also a birder's paradise. Within our first hour, we had spent 15 minutes with a Great Indian hornbill feeding her chicks. Crested serpent eagles were visible in almost every nook and cranny of the forest range. As we moved ahead on the tar road, our driver and I suddenly spotted a leopard crossing the road. By the time we approached it more closely, the leopard vanished into the thicket and I couldn't get any shots of the animal. But something I noticed even with the naked eye was that the leopard had a very short tail, which is very rare in India. It would have been noteworthy had I been able to photograph that leopard. Mr Singh, too, was amazed to see this kind of leopard for the first time. It was around 3 pm, which was an unusual time for a leopard sighting. But that's Rajaji for you, with its vastly high density of leopards.

Despite the minor setback, we kept going farther ahead in search of other leopards. After moving around for two and half hours more, we failed to track down any other leopards and since the light had started to fade, we decided to return to the park gate. During our return journey, we waited for a while near a watering hole where a male leopard had been sighted that very morning, but to no avail. We ended the day with mixed feelings; on the one hand, we were delighted to have spotted an unusual leopard but on the other, we couldn't get any photographs of the animal. Later, we also found that a couple of jeeps had been fortunate enough to see the male leopard near the watering hole, which just goes to show how unpredictable the wild is. I decided to focus on the three upcoming safaris I had left. Early next morning, we reached the safari entrance by 6 am. It was freezing even though it was mid-April, but I had come well-prepared.

In the morning mist, Rajaji's landscape looked ethereal. The majestic sal trees towered over us and apart from the roar of our jeep, the forest was absolutely silent. The silence was finally broken by the mating calls of chital. Before a sighting could happen, Mr Singh decided to take a full round of the forest range in order to understand the mood of the jungle. While on the round, we stopped at a forest *chowki* to enquire if the forest staff had seen any leopards. Just when we were about to take a quick break, Mr Singh got a call from one of his drivers informing him that a male leopard had been sighted feeding on a chital kill. We promptly headed to the place, and saw a couple of jeeps parked on the left side of the road. They told us that the male leopard had ambushed a chital fawn by leaping

FACING PAGE:
A male leopard plays hide & seek in Rajaji

from a tree. Since the leopard was hiding in the bushes, I had to really struggle to spot him. I waited for the leopard to come out into the open, because the shots I was taking weren't turning out great. I decided to make short video clips instead. The leopard was clearly visible to the naked eye and seemed to be staring right back at me.

Suddenly, a herd of wild boars appeared out of nowhere, trying to snatch the kill away from the leopard. But the leopard made sure that it wouldn't be a cakewalk for the boars. Becoming slightly aggressive, the leopard emitted a loud snarl and dragged the kill to a safe hideout. Gauging by the size of his face, the leopard seemed to be a large male. We spent almost 45 minutes there before the leopard completely went back into the thicket after his meal. This time, I was a tad disappointed since I hadn't been able to capture photographs that met my expectations. Seeing the annoyance on my face, Mr Singh assured me not to worry since we still had two more safaris to go. We made our way back to the homestay.

At exactly 2.30 pm, I was picked up by Mr Singh for my afternoon safari. Since it was a Saturday evening, it was relatively more crowded as compared to my previous safaris. This time, Mr Singh was extra determined, and instructed his driver to focus on the male leopard we had sighted on our morning drive. Our chances weren't too bright, but Mr Singh decided to give it our best shot. The driver picked up his speed. As we drove, absorbing the sheer beauty and majesty of the surroundings, I found myself sinking into the magical world of the wild. We continued to move ahead, saw a herd of chital grazing in the sun, but there were no signs of a leopard. Just as we were about to reach our destination, a couple of jeeps seemed to be waiting in the middle of the road. At first, I dismissed them, assuming that they'd spotted some birds nearby. But as we advanced towards them, one of the photographers in those jeeps signalled us to slow down. Suddenly, Mr Singh pointed to the right. Lo and behold! It was a female leopard resting in the open grass. I found out that her name was Mala, courtesy of the garland-like rosette pattern around her neck. I was completely dumbstruck at my first prominent sighting of a Terai leopard. She was so determined to rest that she did not even bother to run away when three more jeeps came in and surrounded her. After a few minutes, Mr Singh exclaimed loudly, indicating that another leopard had appeared. I could barely believe my eyes. The other leopard was Maya, the daughter of Mala. Seeing two leopards in one frame is truly rare, that too in a tiger reserve! I couldn't stop taking photographs. The mother–daughter duo was in no mood to leave the place. I checked the time and it was only 3.45 pm, which meant that there were two more hours left for our evening safari. I made the most of the opportunity and shot some more video clips. This kind of behaviour, especially from a mother–daughter leopard duo, was quite unimaginable. In all my visits to Jhalana since 2016, I had never seen this level of boldness from any female leopard. This is where Terai leopards pose a drastic difference to the urban leopards of Jhalana.

While Mala was busy licking her paws, Maya seemed to be feeling bit lethargic. She yawned multiple times before finally going to her mother. In the meantime, Mala had already changed her position and this time, she came much closer to us, hardly 25 ft away. What a sight! Mr Singh had already told me that whenever a sighting happens in Rajaji, it lasts for a longer period of time, so it could end up becoming slightly monotonous. I could not relate at all, since I was thoroughly enjoying every moment of this incredible sighting.

After an hour or so, Maya jumped up a sal tree with Mala quickly following her and settling down near the

RIGHT: Mala makes an entrance

ABOVE: Eye to eye with a Terai leopard

FACING PAGE: Up close and personal with Mala

ABOVE & RIGHT: Maya looking at a herd of langurs suspiciously

FACING PAGE: Maya moves towards her mother

PG 150–151: Mala guards her daughter

tree. Maya seemed to be a sub-adult female and Mala was behaving exactly like a protective mother. While the sighting was in full swing, we could constantly hear the trumpets of an elephant herd nearby. In the Mohand range, there have been a lot of incidents in the past with elephants charging at the tourist vehicles. I told Mr Singh to be bit careful, to which he smiled and told me not to worry too much.

Around 5.50 pm, the trumpets became more prominent and all the jeeps decided to return since the mother–daughter duo had finally left the place after two whole hours. Within the next five minutes, the elephant herd appeared in front of us and a few tourists in the other jeeps started panicking. The herd had only one tusker, but he was in no mood to charge at us. In fact, it was one of the females with a calf who did a mock charge which led us to leaving that spot immediately. I must admit that I, too, was a little worried. Our brilliant sighting was slightly overshadowed by this alarming conclusion. After the mock charge, our driver drove as fast as he could and we reached the park gate safely.

By the next morning, I had moved past this incident. I decided to focus on my final safari, excited to

LEFT: The lone tusker of Rajaji

see what lay in store after the wonderful sighting of the previous day. This time, I was quite optimistic. Mr Singh was amped up for the climax and he told me to get my camera ready with much aplomb.

Like the previous morning, it was still unusually cold and the weak summer sun had just begun to warm our woollens. Both Mr Singh and his driver leaned over their respective windows to check for pugmarks. After driving around for barely 45 minutes, we saw three jeeps standing at the same point where we had sighted the leopard duo the previous evening. This time, I was fully sure that a brilliant leopard sighting was waiting round the corner for us. I wasn't sure whether it would be Maya, Mala or a different leopard. It turned out to be our very own mother–daughter duo once again. Mala was resting on a tree branch and Maya was trying to stay secluded. Mala was sitting in a place where the light wasn't sufficient, so I decided to focus on Maya who had finally come out in the open. Though it was a Sunday morning, much to my surprise, there were only three jeeps. With hardly any disturbances, the stage was set for me and I was ready to go.

FACING PAGE:
The mighty Rajaji matriarch charges

Maya kept enthralling us with her impishness. In the meantime, Mala had come down from the tree and was sitting right in front of us. She was behaving almost as if she had known us for a long time.

The sun had finally come out but the light conditions were so harsh that I had to make a lot of adjustments in my camera. I was completely awed by the rare friendly nature of the female leopards here. While photographing leopards, we struggle to get them at their best as they are much shyer than tigers. But in Rajaji, this assumption was actually proven wrong. In the past, I had seen a tiger siting right in front of my vehicle, but to see a leopard in this manner was quite extraordinary.

The best part of this morning safari was when Maya came to her mother and started licking her face. The emotional bonding between the mother–daughter duo elevated my Rajaji experience.

The way things seem to be going at Rajaji, I won't be surprised if it topples Jhalana or Kabini to become the best leopard destination in the country. I thanked Mr Singh for this wonderful experience and promised to return to this wonderful place very soon.

FACING PAGE:
Mala, the queen of yawns

PG 158–159:
A game of light and shadow in the Terai

ABOVE AND FACING PAGE: Mother and daughter enjoy quality time together in their Rajaji paradise

BUSTING LEOPARD MYTHS

Among all the big cats of India, leopards have frequented the headlines the most, for reasons such as human–leopard conflicts, livestock depredation, etc. where these felines have been projected as fearsome predators, some people even going as far as calling them 'monsters'. For a clearer picture of this enigmatic beast, wildlife scientist Dr Vidya Athreya, along with renowned naturalist Mr Sanjay Sondhi, published a report in 2017 busting some common myths about leopards.

- Myth: Leopards only live in forests.
- Reality: Being the most adaptable among the big cat species, leopards are distributed across a wide range of habitats—from semi-arid to dense forests; from mountains to urban areas like Mumbai, Jaipur, etc.

LEFT: Staring down the myths

- Myth: Decline in wild prey base along with habitat reduction always leads to human–leopard conflict.
- Reality: In Uttarakhand, there are many such habitats with a smaller wild prey base but practically no human–leopard conflict. Leopards have varied dietary patterns and as a result, they feed on wild as well as domestic prey such as dogs, goats, cows, etc., while co-existing with the human population in the area.
- Myth: Once a leopard gets a taste of human blood, it becomes a man-eater.
- Reality: There is no scientific evidence to prove this assumption. It is true that when leopards get old or badly injured and are unable to hunt on their own, there are chances of them targeting humans, who are much easier to catch. However, it is still widely debated as to how and when a leopard becomes a man-eater.
- Myth: Translocation (human-assisted movement) of leopards solves man–animal conflict.
- Reality: In many cases, it has been observed that translocated leopards later returned to their original site. There are also cases where leopards have created more problems in the translocated site as compared

FACING PAGE:
The most adaptable big cat

to the original. It is said that translocation creates a substantial amount of stress in the leopard, which ultimately leads to aggressiveness in its behaviour, especially towards humans.

- Myth: High leopard density means high conflict.
- Reality: Jhalana has a high leopard density with approximately 2–3 leopards per square kilometre, but there have hardly been cases where leopards have attacked humans.
- Myth: It is said that leopards eat grass on account of indigestion and other illnesses since a significant proportion of plant material has been found in the scat samples of wild felids.
- Reality: As per experts, the consumption of plants is not usually related to gastrointestinal illness but might be inherited behaviour passed down from their ancestors.
- Myth: A leopard can't change its spots.
- Reality: After injuries, the spot patterns of leopards can change at times.

FACING PAGE:
The occasional vegetarian

PG 168–169:
Leopards with their unique rosette patterns

CONCLUSION

Although the leopard population is almost four times the tiger population in India, the probability of seeing a tiger in a national park or wildlife sanctuary is much higher than a leopard sighting. The best example is that of the Ranthambore Tiger Reserve, where leopard sightings are a very rare phenomenon as compared to tigers. However, comparing leopards and tigers is futile, since each cat holds its own. If tigers are masters of strength and brutality, the agility and stealth of leopards are unparalleled. It is unfortunate that the Indian leopard has never been afforded the significance that the tiger has historically held in India. Moreover, due to a scarcity of territory and prey, leopards often face harsh competition from tigers when they share the same habitat and can be forced to leave the area.

LEFT: A bold Rajaji leopard

Although tiger photography has been prevalent in India since the 1960s, up until 20 years ago, it was merely a far-fetched dream for a wildlife enthusiast to be able to photograph a leopard in the wild. It was thought that nocturnal animals like leopards could never be spotted during the day. Now, with the increasing documentation of leopards by wildlife photographers, this perception has changed to a large extent. This has not only created awareness regarding leopard conservation, but has also shed light on lesser-known places with a substantial population of leopards. This is how Jhalana came into the limelight as well, sparking a dialogue around these magnificent animals and the challenges they face. Rajasthan's Project Leopard has played a critical role in this conversation which will hopefully be carried forward by more states in the future.

I come across a lot of debate about whether excessive tourism in Protected Areas like Jhalana hampers the ecosystem. Having studied Jhalana, I would agree to an extent, since I have often seen vehicles chasing down leopards and hyenas, which can be detrimental for all the wildlife inhabiting that area. However, there is a positive side to eco-tourism as well. If implemented in a controlled manner, eco-tourism can be beneficial for conservation since at the end of the day—higher the number of tourists, greater is the revenue generated for wildlife conservation.

After the successful completion of my research work in Jhalana, I believe that more research needs to be conducted in uncharted landscapes that boast of a healthy leopard population, since leopards thriving in different habitats vary in terms of their behavioural and dietary patterns. For research purposes, we conduct studies only in known Protected Areas, and fail to explore what lies beyond. Like Jhalana, there are numerous unmapped places in the country which are inhabited by these majestic big cats. Researchers from esteemed institutions should take initiative and discover more of these lesser-known places. Being such an adaptable big cat, leopards play a crucial role in maintaining a balanced food web in their ecosystem and are classified as a Schedule I species under the Wildlife (Protection) Act, 1972. Hence, it is the need of the hour to initiate further innovative, sustainable steps towards the conservation of this incredible, yet often neglected vulnerable species.

ACKNOWLEDGEMENTS

I am highly thankful to my parents for providing financial support for my wildlife explorations and encouraging me to follow my passion in this field.

I am grateful to my faculty, Dr Erach Bharucha and Dr Shamita Kumar, for the institutional opportunities. I also want to express my endless gratitude to my guide, Dr Kranti Yardi. I would like to especially thank Dr M. Kamalakannan (Sr. Zoological Assistant, Mammal and Osteology section) and the Zoological Survey of India (Kolkata) for helping me with my research analysis.

Thank you, Dr G.V. Reddy and the Rajasthan Forest Department for giving me the opportunity to carry out my field work in Jhalana.

I am eternally indebted to Mr Sumit Juneja, the experienced leopard tracker who guided me through the whole process and my naturalist, Mr Mahendra, for his hard work and dedication.

I will always be grateful to Mr Gurinderjeet Singh, my safari mentor in Rajaji, for persuading me to explore an uncharted part of Rajaji. He is not only a champion tracker but also a gem of a person.

Last but not the least, I would like to thank Niyogi Books for believing in my work and encouraging me to get it published through their esteemed platform.

Other titles from our Nature and Wildlife collection

Wild Wonders of India

A Decade with Tigers:
Supremacy. Solitude. Stripes

Sunderbans:
The Mystic Mangrove

The Great Himalayan National Park: *The Struggle to Save the Western Himalayas*

Sariska
The Tiger Reserve Roars Again

My Encounter with the Big Cat:
And Other Adventures in Ranthambhore

Birds in Paradise:
Keoladeo National Park, Bharatpur

Wildlife in and Around Corbett Tiger Reserve:
A Photographic Guidebook

Flora of the Southern Western Ghats and Palnis:
A Field Guide